Nine Months

Before a Baby Is Born

Miranda Paul
Illustrations by Jason Chin

NEAL PORTER BOOKS
HOLIDAY HOUSE/NEW YORK

For babies and families everywhere
—M. P.

For Olivia
—J. C.

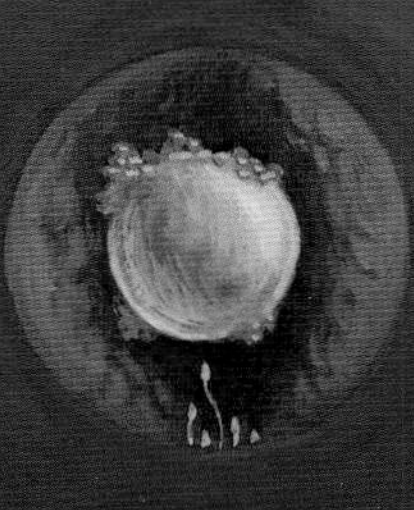

Neal Porter Books

Printed and bound in January 2021 at Toppan Leefung, DongGuan City, China.
The artwork was created with watercolor and gouache on paper.
Book design by Jennifer Browne
www.holidayhouse.com
First Edition
1 3 5 7 9 10 8 6 4 2

Library of Congress Cataloging-in-Publication Data

Names: Paul, Miranda, author. | Chin, Jason, 1978– illustrator.
Title: Nine months : before a baby is born / Miranda Paul ; illustrations by Jason Chin.
Description: First edition. | New York : Holiday House, [2019] | "Neal Porter Books." | Audience: Ages 4–8. | Audience: K to grade 3. | Includes bibliographical references.
Identifiers: LCCN 2018010215 | ISBN 9780823441617 (hardcover)
Subjects: LCSH: Pregnancy—Juvenile literature. | Fetus—Development—Juvenile literature. | Developmental biology—Juvenile literature.
Classification: LCC RG525.5 .P38 2019 | DDC 612.6/4—dc23 LC record available at https://lccn.loc.gov/2018010215

ISBN: 978-0-8234-4161-7 (hardcover)
ISBN: 978-0-8234-4938-5 (paperback)

ELIA, MICHOACÁN

Month One

(Weeks 1 – 4)

Small.
Ball.
The point of a pin.
Then it divides . . .

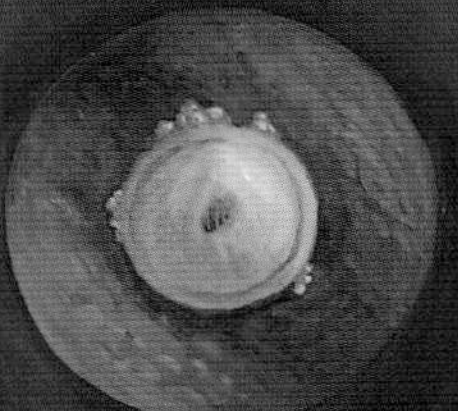

Day 17
Fertilized egg
Actual size: 0.1mm

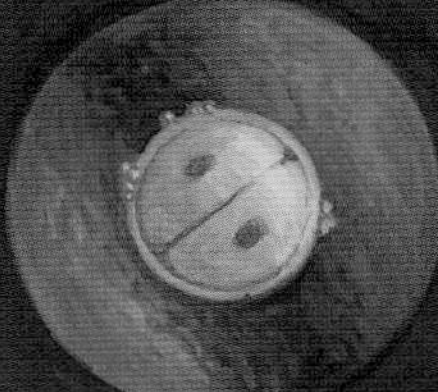

Day 18
2-celled zygote
Actual size: 0.1mm

Day 18 (12–15 hours later)
4-celled zygote
Actual size: 0.1mm

Our story begins.

Month Two
(Weeks 5 – 8)

Starts.
Parts.
Arms, legs . . . *tail, too?*
Hear the heart flutter.

Week 6
Embryo
Actual size: 4mm

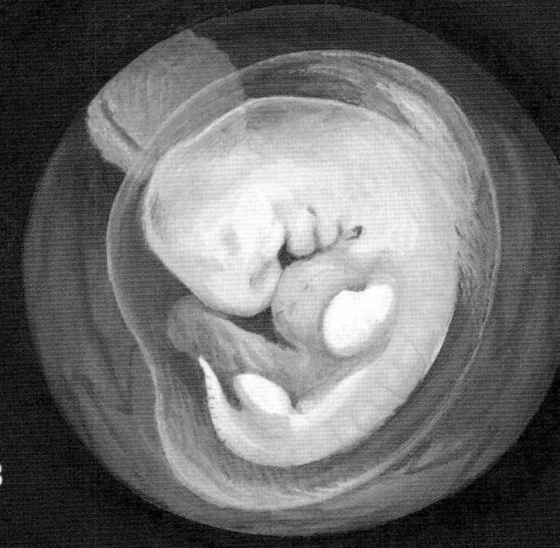

Week 8
Embryo
Actual size: 6mm

Every day, something new.

Month Three
(Weeks 9 – 12)

Grow.
Hello.
The size of a grape.
More features form . . .

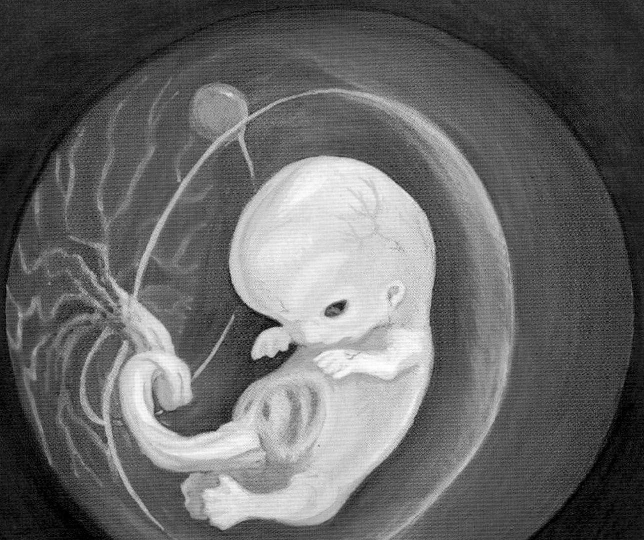

Week 10
Fetus
Actual size: 23mm

See them take shape.

SECOND TRIMESTER

Month Four

(Weeks 13 – 16)

Line.
Spine.
Fine, tiny hair.
Tasting a thumb.

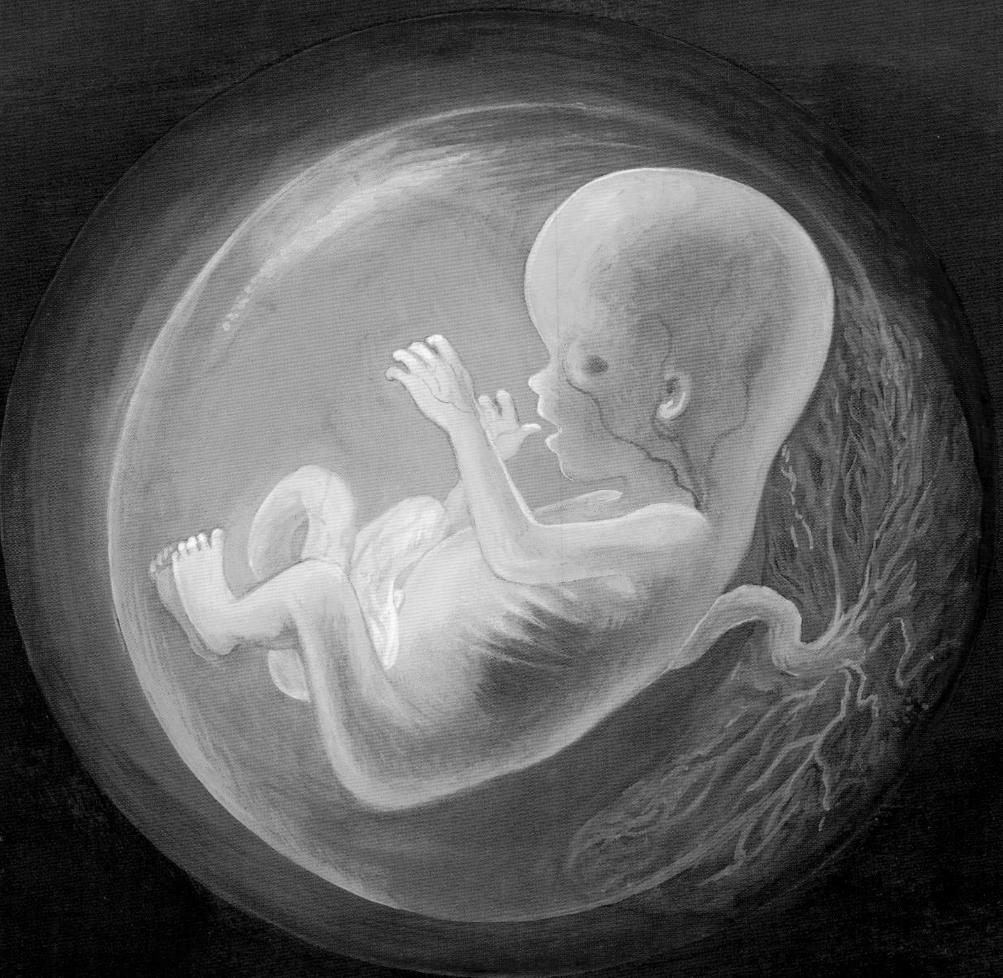

Week 15
Fetus
Actual size

Tasting what's there.

Month Five
(Weeks 17 – 21)

Lips.
Flips.
Curve, dip, and groove.
She has a face.

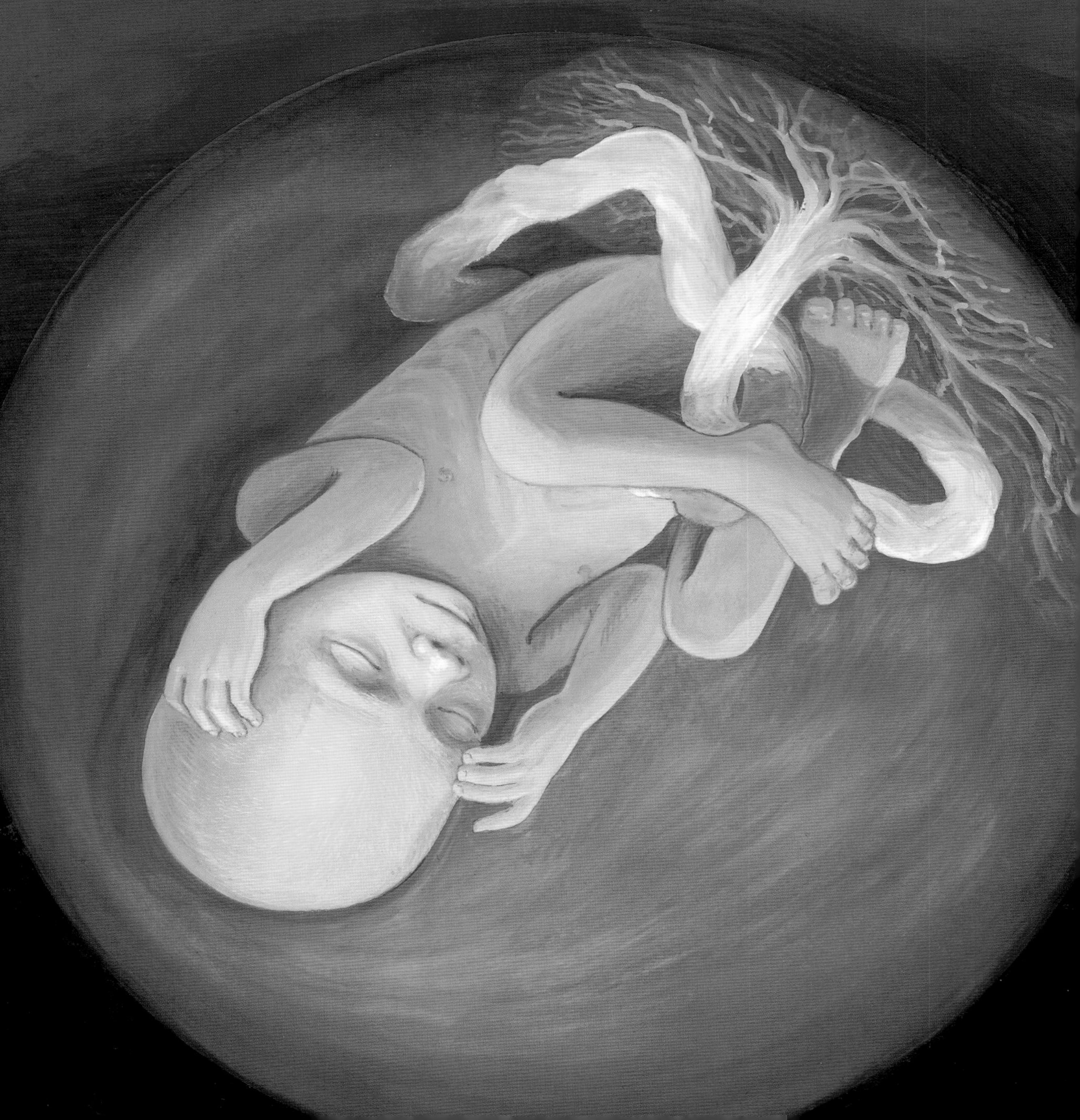

Week 20
Fetus
Actual size

She likes to move!

Month Six

(Weeks 22 – 26)

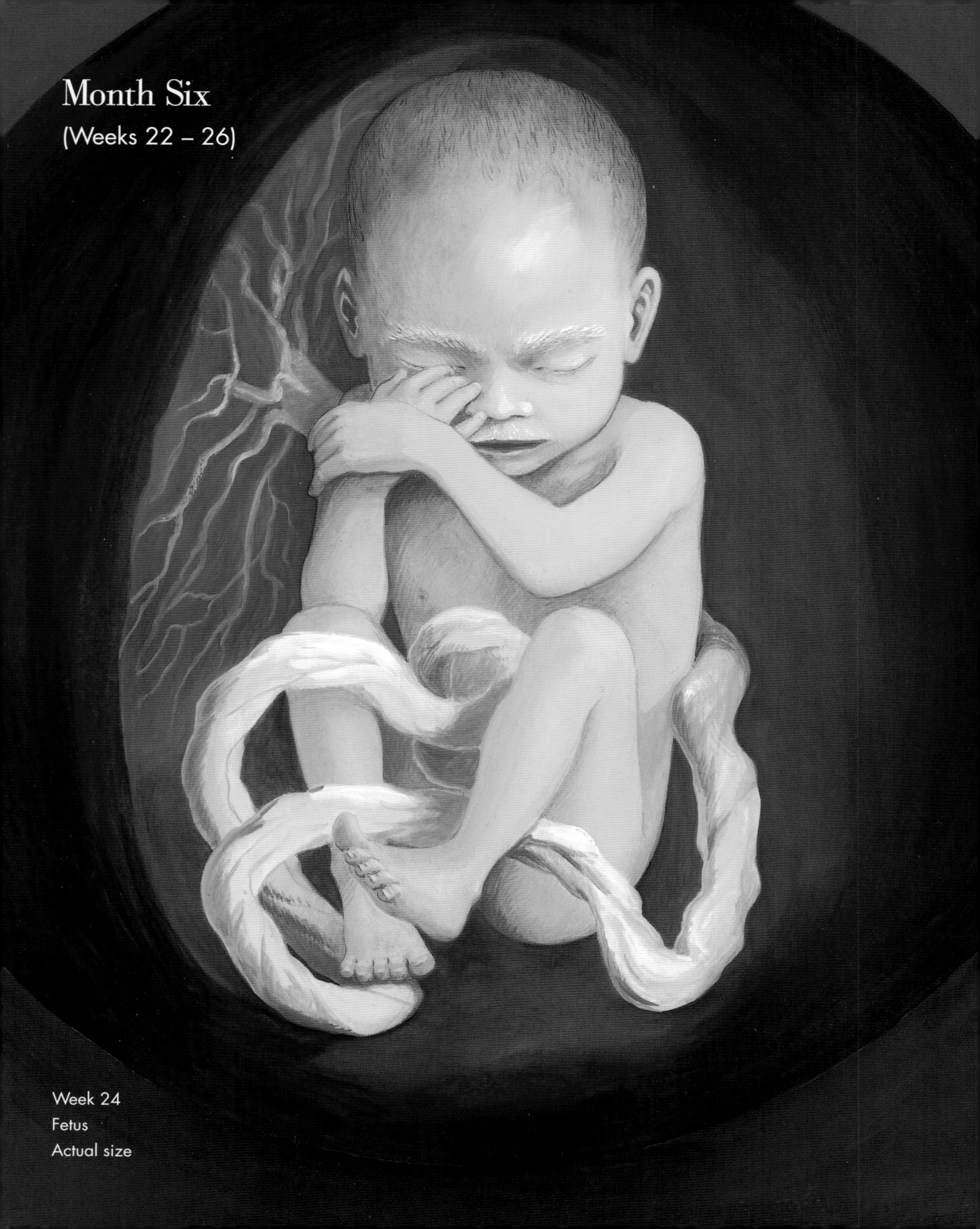

Week 24
Fetus
Actual size

Grasp.
Clasp.
Ears that can hear.
Sing as she listens.
Tell her you're near.

THIRD TRIMESTER

Month Seven

(Weeks 27 – 31)

Week 28
Fetus
Actual size

Lashes.
Flashes.
Systems grow strong.
Feel all those hiccups!
Feel her stretch long.

Months Eight and Nine

(Weeks 32 – birth)

Week 36
Fetus
Actual size

Churn.
Turn.
Not much more room . . .

She's slowing down.

POLICE

She's coming soon.

Birth

Light.
Bright!
Crying and cheer.
Loved ones arrive. . . .

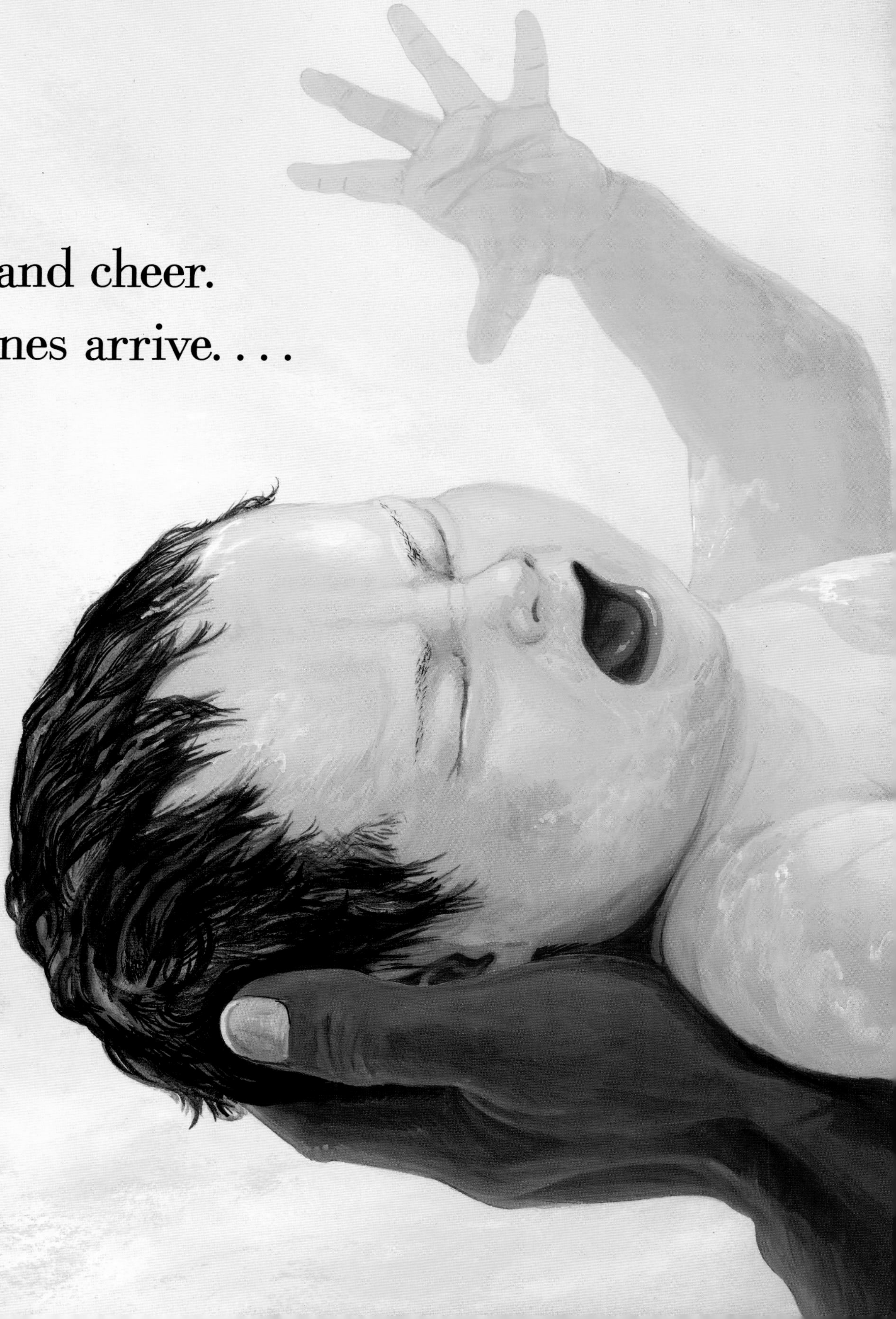

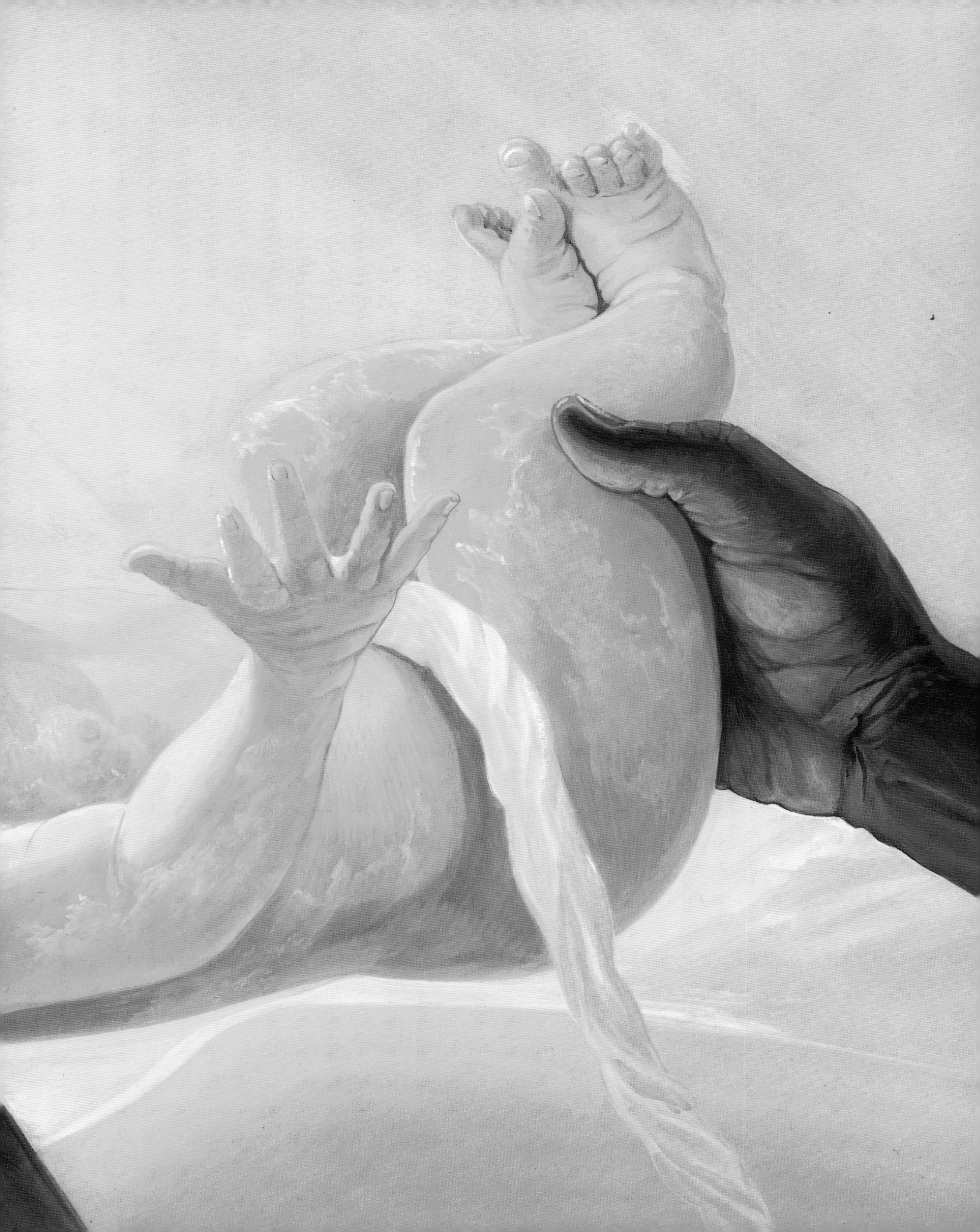

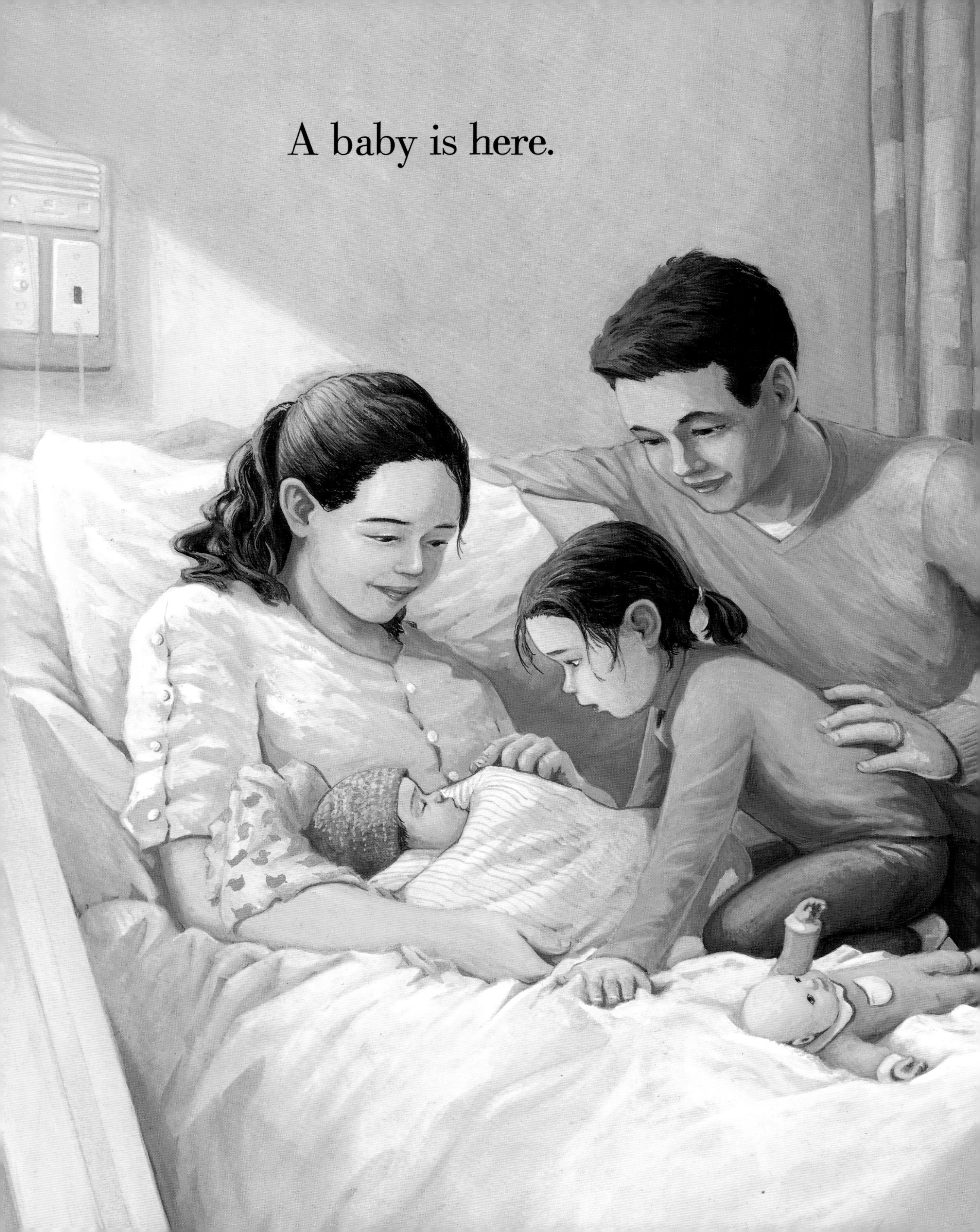

A baby is here.

A GIRL!

MORE ABOUT BABIES

No two human beings are exactly the same. How every baby develops before it's born is also unique. The story and art in this book follow the development, or *gestation*, of one baby for nine calendar months, measured and counted by doctors and scientists as forty weeks. (The count actually begins while the egg is getting ready to be released into the womb, about two weeks before the first captioned picture in this book.) But don't let those specific numbers fool you into thinking it's easy to predict when a baby will arrive—babies are full of wonderful surprises!

Here are some of the developments and changes that happen when babies grow for nine months and are born *full-term.*

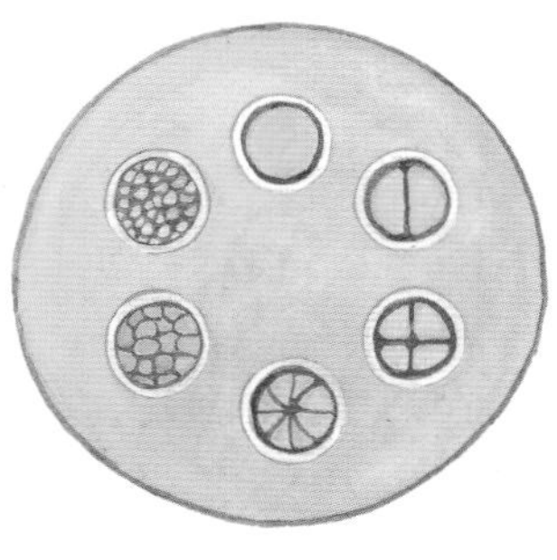

Then it divides. A mother's egg is about the size of a pinpoint, but once it is *fertilized* (after Week 2), it will double into two cells within one day. Two cells become four cells, then eight, and so on. Once the cluster of cells latches on inside the mother, it is called an *embryo.*

Arms, legs . . . *tail, too?* In the second month, little buds that will form the arms and legs become visible. The embryo also has a tail! The tail won't stay very long—it will become part of the lower back or "tailbone" area.

Hear the heart flutter. By Week 6, the heart is pumping! After Week 9, doctors can safely use a special tool called a *Doppler* to hear the heartbeat.

Grow. At Week 9, the embryo is now called a *fetus.* It measures nearly 200 times as big as when it was an egg. (If an average four-year-old were 200 times as tall, they'd stand higher than a 42-story building!)

More features form. By the end of the third month, the fetus looks human. The *placenta*, a flat organ that provides food and nutrients, is well-formed. It is connected from mother to baby by the *umbilical cord*, which will later leave a mark called a "belly button."

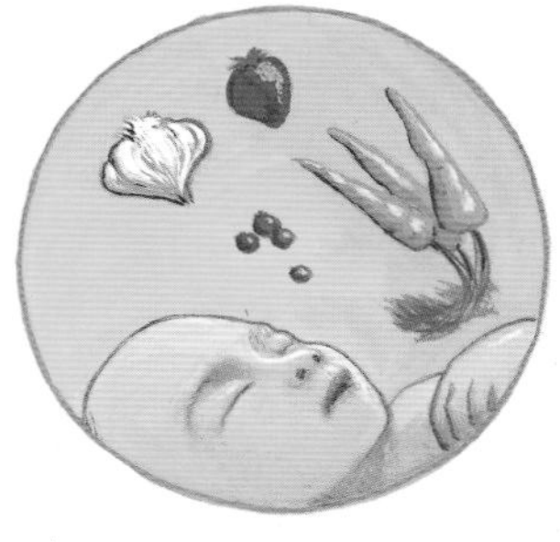

Tasting what's there. The womb is filled with fluid, and the fetus actually gulps mouthfuls of it each day. This *amniotic fluid* is flavored by things the mother eats, such as vanilla, carrots, garlic, or mint. Taste buds form between Weeks 12 and 15, and smell receptors are already formed before Week 12. Scientists aren't sure exactly how much a fetus can smell or taste, but studies suggest that a baby may learn to prefer foods that a mother eats while pregnant.

She has a face. At about 18 to 20 weeks, the doctor will perform an *ultrasound* and print a picture of the baby. The eyelids, eyebrows, nose, and mouth are fully formed. A doctor can usually tell whether the baby has male or female parts.

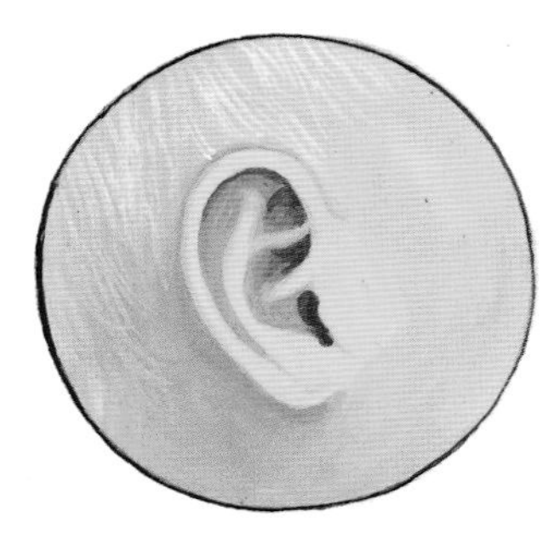

She likes to move! A mother usually feels her baby moving around by the fifth month. The fetus has learned to twist, turn, and even do somersaults. Good thing it still has room to swim around!

Ears that can hear. By the end of the sixth month, the ears have formed inside and out. The fetus can detect the sound of its mother's voice, as well as hear noises from outside the womb.

Systems grow strong. By Week 28, the baby's eyes can sense light. The brain, the center of the *nervous system*, receives many signals. The stomach, part of the *digestive system*, is getting ready to break down food.

Feel all those hiccups! Although the fetus began having hiccups during the fifth month, they're now more frequent and intense. Scientists don't agree on an explanation for why these hiccups happen, but by the seventh month, a family member might be able to feel the hiccups, as well as kicks and stretches, by placing a hand on the mother's belly.

Churn. Turn. Typically by the eighth month a baby begins running out of room. Most will turn their head down and stay that way, which allows for an easier birth. Babies can be born butt-first, or *breech*, but that position is more challenging for both mother and baby.

She's slowing down. With limited space, a baby in its last two months grows more slowly than before, but is still getting fatter and its brain is developing rapidly. Babies also spend time sleeping, and have specific sleep and wake cycles. At Week 35, the lungs get ready to take in air, which the baby will need to survive in the outside world. At Week 37 a baby is considered *full-term*, and birth could happen at any time.

Crying and cheer. When a baby cries shortly after birth, it's a good thing! Crying shows the doctors that the lungs are working. Each newborn is observed and given an *Apgar* score that tells whether it's healthy or needs extra help.

Loved ones arrive. In many cultures, family and friends visit newborn babies. These people—including brothers, sisters, and cousins—will *nurture* them, or help them learn, grow, and succeed as they get older.

WHOA, BABY!

Nine Amazing Things Most Babies Can Do Before They're Born

- Stick out their tongues
- Suck their thumbs
- Swallow and breathe at the same time
- Smell their own mothers
- Recognize voices
- Open and close their eyelids
- Grab on to something
- Do a somersault
- Dream

HUMANS vs. ANIMALS

Humans are part of the animal kingdom. Specifically, we are *mammals*. Baby mammals develop inside their mothers, are born live (instead of hatching), and drink milk. Human babies take nine months to grow. How long does it take for other mammals?

Less than 1 month: opossum, mouse
1 month: rabbit, squirrel
2 months: cat, dog
3–4 months: lion, leopard, tiger
5 months: sheep, goat
6–7 months: deer, black bear, porcupine
8–9 months: gorilla, human
10–11 months: horse, llama, blue whale
12 months: dolphin
13–15 months: camel, giraffe
16–17 months: walrus, rhinoceros
22 months: elephant

averages vary by species

WHAT IF . . . ?

The poem in this story could have been written in as many ways as there are people on Earth. A baby doesn't always grow in exactly this way. Here are a few other ways that babies develop.

What if . . . there are two embryos?

When there are two eggs at the start, and each is fertilized, the mother ends up with *fraternal* twins. Fraternal twins can look very different from each other, and one can be male and the other female. *Identical* twins grow when there's only one original egg but it splits in two, and each half grows into a baby. That's why identical twins look like each other—they're made out of the exact same stuff!

What if . . . there are more than two embryos?

Three babies = triplets
Four babies = quadruplets
Five babies = quintuplets
Six babies = sextuplets
Seven babies = septuplets
Eight babies = octuplets

What if . . . a baby is born early?

Babies rarely come on their *due date*—the day a doctor predicts they might arrive. Each year, about 15 million babies are born before they're 37 weeks old. These *premature* babies often have more growing to do, and some of their systems might not be strong enough yet. To give them extra help, doctors will often place them in a neonatal intensive care unit (NICU). With good medical care, most premature babies over 800 grams (about 2 pounds) will survive. Amazingly, doctors have been able to save some babies who come as early as 23 weeks and weigh as little as 500 grams (about 1 pound).

What if . . . something goes wrong?

Health care professionals help mothers and babies with challenges. But when certain kinds of problems occur with *genes* or *chromosomes*—tiny instruction-giving parts inside the cells—the cells stop growing and the heart doesn't form or stops beating. When this happens before birth (sometimes for unknown reasons), the embryo or fetus dies. This is called a *miscarriage*. The time afterward is very sad for family members. It's important to remember that when this happens, it is not anyone's fault.

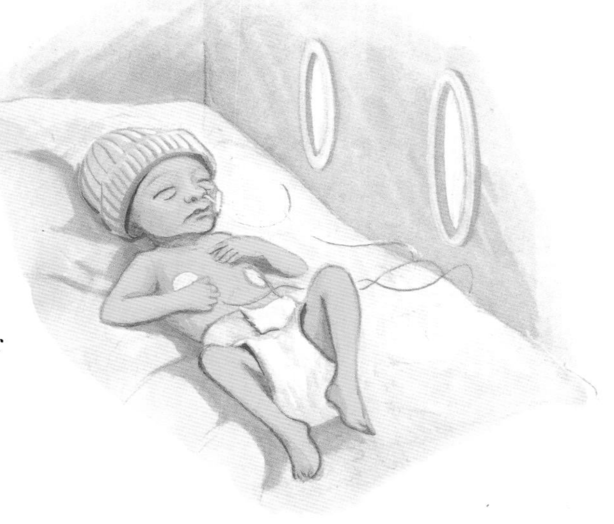

ACKNOWLEDGMENTS

Thanks to Sara Anderson, MD, FACOG, and genetic counselor Theresa Shuck, MS, for their expert reviews of the text and willingness to share their vast knowledge of pregnancy and birth. Any errors or omissions are my own.—M. P.

Thanks to David C. Conway, MD, FACOG, and Jennie Lowell, MD, FACOG, for their help with this project.—J. C.

SELECTED BIBLIOGRAPHY

Brewer, Sarah. *The Pregnant Body Book.* London: Dorling Kindersley, 2011.

Cuda-Kroen, Gretchen. "Baby's Palate and Food Memories Shaped Before Birth." Aired August 8, 2011, on NPR's *Morning Edition*, https://www.npr.org/2011/08/08/139033757/babys-palate-and-food-memories-shaped-before-birth.

Harms, Roger, and Myra Wick. *Mayo Clinic Guide to a Healthy Pregnancy.* Intercourse, PA: Good Books, 2011.

Momont, Harry. "Overview of the Reproductive System." *Merck Veterinary Manual.* Merck Sharp & Dohme, 2018, http://www.merckvetmanual.com/reproductive-system/reproductive-system-introduction/overview-of-the-reproductive-system.

Riley, Laura. *Pregnancy: Your Ultimate Week-by-Week Pregnancy Guide.* Hoboken, NJ: John Wiley & Sons, 2012.

Tallack, Peter. *In the Womb: Witness the Journey from Conception to Birth through Astonishing 3D Images.* Washington, D.C.: National Geographic, 2006.

Witt, Martin, and Klaus Reutter. "Embryonic and early fetal development of human taste buds: A transmission electron microscopical study." *Anatomical Record* 246, No. 4 (1996): 507–523, https://doi.org/10.1002/(SICI)1097-0185(199612)246:4<507::AID-AR10>3.0.CO;2-S.

World Health Organization. "Preterm birth fact sheet." WHO, updated November 2017, http://www.who.int/mediacentre/factsheets/fs363/en/.